Burns and Lambert

The Daily Companion of the sisters of mercy of St. Joseph's

convent

Brighton

Burns and Lambert

The Daily Companion of the sisters of mercy of St. Joseph's convent
Brighton

ISBN/EAN: 9783741172571

Manufactured in Europe, USA, Canada, Australia, Japa

Cover: Foto ©Thomas Meinert / pixelio.de

Manufactured and distributed by brebook publishing software
(www.brebook.com)

Burns and Lambert

The Daily Companion of the sisters of mercy of St. Joseph's

convent

THE

DAILY COMPANION

OF

THE SISTERS OF MERCY

OF

ST. JOSEPH'S CONVENT,

BRIGHTON.

––––––––

LONDON:
BURNS & LAMBERT, PORTMAN STREET,
PORTMAN SQUARE.
1862.

THE

DAILY COMPANION.

✠ In the name of the Father, &c.

In the name of our Lord Jesus Christ crucified, I will now arise. O my God, to thee do I
watch at break of day; bless me, protect and
direct me this day and for ever. Amen.

Putting on the Habit.

Clothe my soul, O Lord, with the nuptial
garment of charity, that, pure and undefiled, I
may carry it before thy judgment-seat.

Cincture.

O my dear Lord Jesus Christ, who for my
sake becamest obedient unto death, even the
death of the cross, grant me the true spirit of
religious obedience.

Beads and Cross.

O Jesus, meek and humble of heart, teach
me to deny myself, to take up my cross daily,
and to follow thee.

O Mary, refuge of sinners, pray for me.

D

Coif.

Place thyself, O Lord, as a seal on my forehead, that I may be of the number of those who follow the Lamb.

Guimpe.

Create a clean heart in me, O God, and renew a right spirit within my bowels.

Veil.

Place on my head, O Lord, the helmet of salvation.

O Immaculate Virgin, obtain for me purity of soul and body.

Church Cloak.

Restore to me, O Lord, the robe of immortality, which I lost in the prevarication of my first parents.

Prepare for the morning exercise by a short recollection of what imperfections you are most subject to, and of what purposes ought to be made against them.
Take holy water, and on your knees say:

I adore thee, O my God, and I thank thee for all thy benefits. I offer thee my heart, with all my affections and resolutions, and all the thoughts, words, actions, and sufferings of this day, in union with the loving oblation which my Saviour made of himself to thee on the tree of the cross. I implore thy help and blessing, that I may serve thee faithfully; and

I desire to gain all the indulgences I may be partaker of, by prayers or other good works.

O my most compassionate Lord and Saviour Jesus Christ, I humbly beseech thee to look on me this day with pity, and grant me grace to be pleasing and acceptable to thee, even for one moment. Amen.

Nos cum prole pia benedicat Virgo Maria.

My good angel and holy patrons, pray for me.

O sweet Jesus, that every hour of my life, and every motion of my heart, might praise thy sacred Majesty! Oh, that every step I take might draw me nearer and nearer to thy love!

BEFORE MEDITATION.

Come, Holy Ghost, take possession of our hearts, and kindle in them the fire of Divine love.

Send forth thy Spirit, and they shall be created, and thou wilt renew the face of the earth.

Let us pray.

O eternal Father, shed upon us, we beseech thee, the plenitude of thy Divine Spirit, and give us an entire and perfect submission to the inspirations of thy grace. We renounce from the bottom of our hearts every thought and affection which may withdraw us from thy adorable presence; and we most earnestly implore, through the merits and sufferings of our Lord Jesus Christ, and the intercession of his sacred and Immaculate Mother, our angel

guardians, and patron saints, that this meditation may conduce to thy glory and to our eternal salvation.   Amen.

MORNING PRAYER.

I adore thee, O my God and Creator, with
the most profound respect, and I acknowledge
thee to be the Source of my being, and Author
of all the blessings I have received, which are
so great and numerous that I can never suffi-
ciently express my obligations.   I therefore
thank thee, O my God, for having created me
out of nothing, after thy own likeness, and for
the enjoyment of thyself in heaven; for having redeemed me with the Blood of thy only
Son; for having called me to the true faith;
for having delivered me from so many dangers,
which might have ruined me both for this and
the next world; for having prevented me with
innumerable graces; and for having preserved
me this night past from sin and sudden death.
But to my confusion I must confess, O God,
that I have repaid thy benefits with nothing
but sin and ingratitude; and this it is that
causes my sorrow, and obliges me to beg pardon of thee, with a heart sensibly touched
and sincerely troubled at the sight of my offences; and I beg these sentiments of sorrow
may be still more lively, that to the utmost
of my power I may make amends for my ingratitude and offences.

I offer thee my heart, my thoughts, my actions, and all afflictions that may befall me this

day, whether by the express orders of thy justice, or by the permission of thy providence, in union with the actions, sufferings, and merits of our Lord Jesus Christ. But as I stand in great need of thy powerful grace to sanctify all my actions, and to make a right use of suffering, I ask for it through the merits of my Redeemer; and since these merits are of infinite value, and he has given me a title to them, I firmly hope that thou wilt grant me my request. By the help of this same grace, I resolve to employ my best endeavours to serve thee faithfully this day, exactly to discharge my duties, and carefully to avoid whatever may offend thee, but especially to decline the sins to which I am most subject, and which most withstand thy designs for my sanctification. Through Jesus Christ our Lord. Amen.

Our Father. Hail Mary. Creed.

O holy Virgin, Mother of God, my Advocate and Patroness, pray for thy poor servant; prove thyself a Mother to me.

And thou, O blessed spirit, my Guardian Angel, whom God, in his mercy, has appointed to watch over me, intercede for me this day, that I may be preserved from all sin and danger.

Glorious St. Joseph, my blessed Patrons, and all you, happy Saints, pray for me, that I may serve God faithfully in this life as you have done, and, with you, glorify him eternally in heaven. Amen.

Examen.

(At a quarter to twelve.)

PRAYER BEFORE THE EXAMEN OF CONSCIENCE.

My God, I adore thee, I thank thee with my whole heart and soul, for all thy mercies to me a sinner. Thou hast created me for thy glory, redeemed me with thy precious Blood, called me to the true faith, and, with most unspeakable goodness, chosen me for thy spouse, permitting me to dwell under the same roof with thyself and thy chosen servants. O my soul, bless the Lord, and let all that is within thee praise and magnify his holy Name. He has done all things for me; I will praise and magnify him for ever.

O Divine Spirit of light and truth, enlighten me, that I may know myself.

O my God, illuminate my darkness.

Did I, on awaking, make the sign of the cross, and give my first thoughts to God?

Did I dress myself with diligence and modesty, take holy water, and on my knees offer myself and the actions of the day to Almighty God?

How did I enter the choir, and make my meditation?

Can I now remember which point excited me most to serve God faithfully during the day?

How did I say morning prayers and recite the Holy Office?

Did I recollect that I was joining with the Angels and Saints in the Divine praises?

How did I assist at Mass?

Did I beg of God with fervour and confidence the graces I stand in need of?

What was my preparation for, and thanks-giving after, Holy Communion?

How did I act in the refectory?

Did I remember that it was the will of God I was going to accomplish?

Did I practise some small self-denial?

Was I attentive to the spiritual lecture?

How has my time been employed since?

Have I thought of God, or made any act of virtue?

Did I perform all my actions with a pure in-tention of pleasing God?—[Here reflect in a special manner on *that virtue* you are trying to acquire, or *that fault* you are trying to era-dicate, and which is the subject of your par-ticular Examen. Think of the example your Blessed Lord gives you in that particular, and resolve to conform yourself thereto.]

Having concluded your Examen, present yourself before your Divine Lord as one sick to his hea-venly Physician; discovering all your wounds with confidence, that he may apply thereto the sacred balm of his adorable Blood. Say with St. Austin:

O good Jesus, take possession anew of my whole soul, and all that belongs to thee; re-vive therein the traces of thy own sacred Image, obscured by sin, and efface every stain of vice and imperfection.

Cast yourself into the burning furnace of your Saviour's Sacred Heart, there to purify your soul, and with sincere contrition say :

O eternal God, prostrate at thy sacred feet, and penetrated with the most sincere and lively contrition, I implore thy pardon for all the sins of my life, particularly for those I have had the misfortune to commit this day. I detest them all in general, and each one in particular; and I wish with all my heart and soul that I had never been so unhappy as to lose the precious treasure of thy grace and friendship. I firmly purpose, with thy Divine grace and assistance, to confess, to correct my vicious inclinations, and to atone for my transgressions.

Angelus or Regina, &c., and three Glorias.

ACTS.

O almighty and eternal God, grant unto us an increase of faith, hope, and charity; and that we may deserve to obtain what thou hast promised, make us love and practise what thou hast commanded. Through Jesus Christ our Lord. Amen.

My God, I am heartily sorry for having offended thee; I detest my sins most sincerely, because they displease thee, my God, who art so deserving of all my love, for thine infinite goodness and most amiable perfections; and I

firmly purpose, by thy holy grace, never more
to offend thee.

My God, I firmly believe thou art one only
God, the Creator and Sovereign Lord of heaven and earth, infinitely great and infinitely
good. I firmly believe that in thee, one only
God, there are three Divine Persons, really
distinct, and equal in all things,—the Father,
the Son, and the Holy Ghost. I firmly believe
that Jesus Christ, God the Son, became man ;
that he was conceived by the Holy Ghost, and
was born of the Virgin Mary ; that he suffered
and died on a Cross, to redeem and save us;
that he arose the third day from the dead ;
that he ascended into heaven; that he will come
at the end of the world to judge mankind;
that he will reward the good with eternal happiness, and condemn the wicked to the everlasting pains of hell. I believe these and all
other articles which the holy Catholic Church
proposes to our belief, because thou, my God,
the infallible Truth, hast revealed them, and
thou hast commanded us to hear the Church,
which is the pillar and the ground of truth. In
this faith I am firmly resolved, by thy holy
grace, to live and die.

My God, who hast graciously promised every
blessing, even heaven itself, through Jesus
Christ, to those who keep thy commandments,
relying on thy infinite power, goodness, and
mercy, and on thy sacred promises, to which
thou art always faithful, I confidently hope to

obtain pardon of all my sins, grace to serve
thee faithfully in this life, and eternal happiness in the next, through Jesus Christ our
Lord.

O my God, I love thee with my whole heart
and soul, and, above all things, because thou
art infinitely good and perfect, and most worthy
of all my love; and for thy sake, I love my
neighbour as myself. Mercifully grant, O my
God, that, having loved thee on earth, I may
love and enjoy thee for ever in heaven. Amen.

Litany of the Holy Name.

Lord, have mercy on us.
Christ, have mercy on us.
Lord, have mercy on us.
Christ, hear us.
Christ, graciously hear us.
God the Father, of heaven,
God the Son, Redeemer of the world,
God the Holy Ghost,
Holy Trinity, one God,
Jesus, Son of the living God,
Jesus, Splendour of the Father,
Jesus, Brightness of eternal light,
Jesus, King of glory,
Jesus, Sun of justice,
Jesus, Son of the Virgin Mary,
Jesus, most amiable,
Jesus, most admirable,
Jesus, mighty God,

Have mercy on us.

Litany

OF THE

MOST HOLY NAME OF JESUS.

An Indulgence of three hundred days was granted by Rescript, dated April 28, 1864, to the Faithful in England for the devout recitation of the Litany of the Most Holy Name, by our Most Holy Father Pope Pius IX., who at the same time prohibited any form but that of which the following is a translation, authorised by the Bishops.

Kyrie eleison.	Lord, have mercy on us.
Christe eleison.	Christ, have mercy on us.
Kyrie eleison.	Lord, have mercy on us.
Jesu, audi nos.	Jesus, hear us.
Jesu, exaudi nos.	Jesus, graciously hear us.
Pater de cœlis Deus,	God the Father, of heaven.
Fili Redemptor mundi Deus,	God the Son, Redeemer of the world,
Spiritus Sancte Deus,	God the Holy Ghost,
Sancta Trinitas, unus Deus,	Holy Trinity, one God,
Jesu, Fili Dei vivi,	Jesus, Son of the living God,
Jesu, splendor Patris,	Jesus, splendour of the Father,
Jesu, candor lucis æternæ,	Jesus, brightness of eternal light,
Jesu, Rex gloriæ,	Jesus, King of glory,
Jesu, sol justitiæ,	Jesus, Sun of justice,
Jesu, Fili Mariæ Virginis,	Jesus, Son of the Virgin Mary,
Jesu amabilis,	Jesus, most amiable,
Jesu admirabilis,	Jesus, most admirable,
Jesu, Deus fortis,	Jesus, mighty God,
Jesu, Pater futuri sæculi,	Jesus, Father of the world

Miserere nobis.

Have mercy on us.

Jesu, magni consilii Angele,
Jesus, Angel of great counsel,

Jesu potentissime,
Jesus, most powerful,

Jesu patientissime,
Jesus, most patient,

Jesu obedientissime,
Jesus, most obedient,

Jesu, mitis et humilis corde,
Jesus, meek and humble of heart,

Jesu, amator castitatis,
Jesus, lover of chastity,

Jesu, amator noster,
Jesus, lover of us,

Jesu, Deus pacis,
Jesus, God of peace,

Jesu, auctor vitæ,
Jesus, Author of life,

Jesu, exemplar virtutum,
Jesus, example of virtues,

Jesu, zelator animarum,
Jesus, zealous lover of souls,

Jesu, Deus noster,
Jesus, our God,

Jesu, refugium nostrum,
Jesus, our refuge,

Jesu, pater pauperum,
Jesus, Father of the poor,

Jesu, thesaurus fidelium,
Jesus, treasure of the faithful,

Jesu, bone pastor,
Jesus, Good Shepherd,

Jesu, lux vera,
Jesus, true light,

Jesu, sapientia æterna,
Jesus, eternal wisdom.

Jesu, bonitas infinita,
Jesus, infinite goodness,

Jesu, via et vita nostra,
Jesus, our way and our life,

Jesu, gaudium Angelorum,
Jesus, joy of Angels,

Jesu, Rex Patriarcharum,
Jesus, King of Patriarchs,

Jesu, Magister Apostolorum,
Jesus, Master of Apostles,

Jesu, Doctor Evangelistarum,
Jesus, Teacher of Evangelists,

Jesu, fortitudo Martyrum,
Jesus, strength of Martyrs,

Jesu, lumen Confessorum,
Jesus, light of Confessors,

Jesu, puritas Virginum.
Jesus, purity of Virgins,

Jesu, corona Sanctorum
Jesus, Crown of all Saints,

Miserere nobis.

Have mercy on us.

Propitius esto,
Exaudi nos, Jesu.
Ab omni malo,
Ab omni peccato,
Ab ira tua,
Ab insidiis diaboli,

A spiritu fornicationis,

A morte perpetua,
A neglectu inspirationum tuarum,
Per mysterium sanctæ In-carnationis tuæ,
Per nativitatem tuam,
Per infantiam tuam,
Per divinissimam vitam tuam,
Per labores tuos,
Per agoniam et passionem tuam,
Per crucem et derelictio-nem tuam,
Per languores tuos,

Per mortem et sepultu-ram tuam.
Per resurrectionem tuam,

Per ascensionem tuam,
Per gaudia tua,
Per gloriam tuam,
Agnus Dei, qui tollis pec-cata mundi,

Parce nobis, Jesu.
Agnus Dei, qui tollis pec-cata mundi,

Exaudi nos Jesu.

Libera nos, Jesu.

Be merciful unto us,
Graciously hear us, O Jesus.
From all evil,
From all sin,
From Thy wrath,
From the snares of the devil,
From the spirit of un-cleanness,
From everlasting death,
From the neglect of Thy Inspirations,
Through the mystery of Thy holy Incarnation,
Through Thy Nativity.
Through Thine infancy,
Through Thy most divine life,
Through Thy labours,
Through Thine agony and passion,
Through Thy Cross and dereliction,
Through Thy faintness and weariness.
Through Thy death an: burial,
Through Thy resurrec-tion,
Through Thine ascension.
Through Thy joys,
Through Thy glory,
Lamb of God, who takest away the sins of the world,
Spare us, O Jesus.
Lamb of God, who takest away the sins of the world.
Graciously hear us, O Jesus.

Jesus, deliver us.

Agnus Dei, qui tollis pec-
cata mundi,

Miserere nobis, Jesu.
Jesu, audi nos.
Jesu, exaudi nos,

Lamb of God, who takest
away the sins of the
world,

Have mercy on us, O Jesus.
Jesus, hear us.
Jesus, graciously hear us.

Oremus.

Domine Jesu Christe, qui
dixisti: Petite, et accipietis;
quærite, et invenietis; pul-
sate, et aperietur vobis:
quæsumus, da nobis peten-
tibus divinissimi tui amoris
affectum, ut te toto corde,
ore et opere diligamus, et a
tua nunquam laude cesse-
mus.

Sancti Nominis tui, Do-
mine, timorem pariter et
amorem fac nos habere per-
petuam, quia nunquam tua
gubernatione destituis quos
in soliditate tuæ dilectionis
instituis. Per Dominum.

Let us pray.

O Lord Jesus Christ, who
hast said: Ask, and ye shall
receive; seek, and ye shall
find; knock, and it shall be
opened unto you; give, we
beseech Thee, to us who
ask, the grace of Thy most
divine love, that with all
our heart, words and works,
we may love Thee, and
never cease to praise Thee.

Make us, O Lord, to have
a perpetual fear and love of
Thy holy Name, for Thou
never failest to govern those
whom Thou dost solidly
establish in Thy love.
Through Jesus Christ our
Lord. Amen.

London: Burns and Oates, 17 and 18 Portman Street.

knook,. and it shall be opened to you ;" mercifully attend to our supplications, and grant us
the gift of Divine charity, that we may ever love
thee with our whole hearts, and never cease
from praising thy holy Name. Who livest and
reignest one God, world without end. Amen.

May the Divine assistance remain always
with us. Amen.

And may the souls of the faithful departed,
through the mercy of God, rest in peace.
Amen.

After Matins and Lauds, *De Profundis* and

Litany for a Happy Death.

O Lord Jesus, God of goodness and Father
of mercies, I approach to thee with a contrite
and humble heart ; to thee I recommend the
last hour of my life, and the decision of my
eternal doom.

When my feet, benumbed with death,
shall admonish me that my mortal course
is drawing to an end,

When my eyes, dim and troubled at the
approach of death, shall fix themselves on
thee, my last and only support,

When my face, pale and livid, shall inspire the beholders with pity and dismay,

When my hair, bathed in the sweat of
death, and stiffening on my head, shall for-
bode my approaching end,

When my ears, soon to be for ever shut

Merciful Jesus, have mercy on me.

to the discourse of men, shall be open to hear the irrevocable decree which is to cut me off from the number of the living,

When my imagination, agitated by dreadful spectres, shall be sunk in an abyss of anguish,

When my soul, affrighted with the sight of my iniquities and terror of thy judgments, shall have to fight against the Angel of darkness, who will endeavour to conceal thy mercies from my eyes, and to plunge me into despair,

When my poor heart, yielding to the pressure, and exhausted by its frequent struggles against the enemy of its salvation, shall feel the pangs of death,

When the last tear, the forerunner of my dissolution, shall drop from my eyes, receive it as a sacrifice of expiation for my sins; grant that I may expire the victim of penance; and in that dreadful moment,

When I shall have lost the use of my senses; when the world shall have vanished from my sight; when my agonising soul shall feel the sorrows of death,

When my last sigh shall summon my soul to burst from the embraces of the body, and to spring to thee on the wings of impatience and desire,

When my soul, trembling on my lips, shall bid adieu to the world, and leave my body lifeless, pale, and cold, receive this

Merciful Jesu, have mercy on me.

separation as a homage which I willingly pay to thy Divine Majesty; and in that last moment of my mortal life,

When at length my soul, admitted to thy presence, shall first behold thy Majesty, reject me not, but receive me into thy bosom, where I may for ever sing thy praises; and in that moment, when eternity shall begin to me,

Merciful Jesus, &c.

Let us pray.

O God, who hast doomed all to die, but hast concealed from all the hour of their death; grant that I may pass my days in the practice of holiness and justice, and that I may deserve to quit this world in the peace of a good conscience and in the embraces of thy love, through Jesus Christ our Lord. Amen.

After Compline on Mondays,
Litany of the Dead.

Lord, have mercy on us.
Lord, have mercy on us.
Christ, have mercy on us.
Christ, have mercy on us.
Lord, have mercy on us.
Lord, have mercy on us.
Jesus, receive our prayers.
Lord Jesus, grant our petitions.
O God the Father, Creator of the world,
Have mercy on the souls of the faithful departed.

O God the Son, Redeemer of mankind,
Deliver the souls of the faithful departed.
O God the Holy Ghost, Perfecter of the
elect,
*Accomplish the bliss of the souls of the faithful
departed.*
O sacred Trinity, Three Persons and one
God,
Give rest to the souls of the faithful departed.
Blessed Virgin Mary, who, by a special privilege of grace, wast triumphantly assumed
into the kingdom of thy Son,
Blessed Angels, who, ordering aright the
first act of your will, were immediately
settled in an unchangeable state of felicity,
Blessed Patriarchs, whose spirits were filled
with joy when the Desired of all nations
brought redemption to your long captivity,
Blessed Prophets, who, having patiently
awaited the coming of the Messias, were
at length refreshed with the happy visit
of his Divine Person,
O all you blessed Saints, who, after the glorious resurrection of your Saviour, were
by him translated from the bosom of Abraham to the clear vision of God,
Blessed Apostles, who, at the last and terri-
ble day, shall sit on the twelve thrones,
judging the tribes of Israel,
Blessed Disciples of our Lord, who, following his sacred steps in the narrow path of

Pray for the souls of the faithful departed.

perfection, went straight on to the heavenly Jerusalem,

Blessed Martyrs, who, passing through the Red Sea of your own blood, without journeying through a tedious wilderness, entered immediately into the land of Promise,

Blessed Confessors, who, despising the vanities here below, and placing your affections entirely on the joys above, are already arrived at the full possession of all your wishes,

Blessed Virgins, who, watching continually with your lamps prepared, were ready at the first voice of the chaste Spouse of heaven to enter with him into the marriage-chamber,

O all you holy Saints, who, not retaining at your death the least irregular adherence to any creature, were perfectly capable of an immediate union with your Creator,

Be merciful, O Lord,

And pardon their sins.

Be merciful, O Lord,

And hear our prayers.

From the shades of death, where they sit deprived of the blissful light of thy countenance,

Deliver them, O Lord.

From the evils to which their defective mortifications in this world have exposed them in the other,

Deliver them, O Lord.

Pray for the souls of the faithful departed.

From thine anger, which now too late they grieve to have provoked by their negligence and ingratitude,

From the bonds of sin, wherein they remain entangled by the disorder of their affections,

From the pains of purgatory, justly inflicted on them as the proper effects of their sins,

From that dreadful prison, whence there is no release till they have paid the last farthing,

From all their torments, incomparably greater than the sharpest pains of this life,

By the multitude of thy mercies, which have always shown compassion on the frailties of human nature,

By the infinite merits of thy death upon the Cross, where thou reconciledst the world to thy Father,

By thy victorious descent into hell, to break asunder the chains of death, and free such as were imprisoned,

By thy glorious resurrection from the grave, when thou openedst the kingdom of heaven to believers,

By thy triumphant ascension into heaven, when thou ledst captivity captive, and promisedst to prepare a place for thy servants,

By thy dreadful coming to judge the world, when the works of every one shall be tried by fire,

Deliver them, O Lord.

We sinners,
Beseech thee hear us.

That it would please thee to hasten the day
of visiting thy faithful detained in the re-
ceptacles of sorrow, and transport them to
the city of eternal peace,

That it would please thee to shorten the
time of expiation of their sins, and graciously admit them into thy holy sanctuary, where no unclean thing can enter,

That it would please thee, through the prayers and alms of thy Church, and especially
the inestimable Sacrifice of thy holy Altar, to receive them into the tabernacles
of rest, and crown their longing hopes with
everlasting fruition,

That the blessed vision of Jesus may comfort them, and the glorious light of his
cross shine upon them,

That thy holy Angels may bring them into
the land of the living, and the glorious
Queen of Saints present them before thy
throne,

That the venerable Patriarchs may meet
them, and all the ancient Prophets rejoice
to see them,

That the sacred college of Apostles may
open to them the gates of bliss, and the
victorious army of Martyrs conduct them
to thy palace,

That the blessed company of Confessors may
place them in seats of eternal glory, and

the chaste train of Virgins, with heavenly
anthems, congratulate their reception,

That the whole triumphant Church may celebrate the jubilee of their deliverance;
and all the choirs of Angels sing hymns of
joy, for their new and never-ending felicity,

That, in the midst of all these triumphs, the
souls that are delivered may themselves
adore the glorious Author of their happiness, and, in their white robes, eternally
sing, Alleluia! salvation to our God, who
sitteth upon the throne, and to the Lamb
that redeemed us by his Blood, and made
us kings to reign with him for ever,

We beseech thee, hear us.

Son of God,

O Lamb of God, who wilt come with glory to
judge the living and the dead,

Give rest to the souls of the faithful departed.

O Lamb of God, at whose presence the earth
shall be moved, and the heavens melt away,

Give rest to the souls of the faithful departed.

O Lamb of God, in whose blessed book of life
all their names are written,

*Give eternal rest to the souls of the faithful de-
parted.*

THE ANTIPHON.

Deliver us, O Lord, and all thy faithful, in
that day of terror, when the sun and moon shall
be darkened, and the stars fall down from heaven; in that day of calamity and amazement,
when Heaven itself shall shake, the pillars of

the earth be moved, and the glorious majesty of Jesus come with innumerable angels to judge the world by fire.

℣. Deliver us, O Lord, in that dreadful day.

℟. And place us with the blessed at thy right hand for ever.

℣. O Lord, hear my prayer.

℟. And let my cry come to thee.

Almighty God, with whom do live the spirits of the perfect, and in whose holy custody are deposited the souls of all those that depart hence in an inferior degree of thy grace, who, being by their imperfect charity rendered unworthy of thy presence, are detained in a state of grief and suspended hopes; as we bless thee for the saints already admitted to thy glory, so we humbly offer our prayers for thy afflicted servants, who continually wait and sigh after the day of their deliverance : pardon their sins, supply their unpreparedness, and wipe away the tears from their eyes, that they may see thee, and in thy glorious light eternally rejoice. Through Jesus Christ, &c.

O eternal God, who, besides the general precept of charity, hast commanded a particular respect to parents, kindred, and benefactors ; grant, we beseech thee, that, as they were the instruments by which thy Providence bestowed on us our birth, education, and innumerable other blessings, so our prayers may be the means to obtain for them a speedy release from their excessive sufferings, and free admittance to thine infinite joys. Through, &c.

Most wise and merciful Lord, who hast ordained this life as a passage to the future, confining our repentance to the time of our pilgrimage here, and reserving for hereafter the state of punishment and reward; vouchsafe us thy grace, who are yet alive, and still have opportunity of reconciliation with thee, so to watch over all our actions, and correct every least deviation from the true way to heaven, that we be neither surprised with our sins uncancelled, nor with our duties imperfect; but when our bodies go down into the grave, our souls may ascend to thee, and dwell for ever in the mansions of eternal felicity. Through Jesus Christ, our Lord and only Saviour. Amen.

ON FRIDAY, AT THREE O'CLOCK.

Adorable Heart of Jesus! hypostatically united to the Eternal Word, ever present in the Holy Eucharist, receive my homage, and the tribute of adoration which I here bring, prostrate at the throne of thy glory. Mayest thou ever be reverenced and adored by all creatures! May the raising of hands, bending of knees, prostrations of body, practised in our devotions; may the prayers, vows, and sacrifices of thy servants, be ever agreeable and ac-

ceptable to thee; may the Angels in heaven
ever adore thee; and may the hearts of all the
faithful, especially that of the Most Blessed
Virgin, ever breathe out in thy honour a most
sweet odour and perfume of love, esteem, and
respect! Sweet Jesus, receive this act of adoration! May it be acceptable in thy sight from
my hands, and those of thy servants of this
association, whom I particularly recommend to
thee.

Our Father, Hail Mary, five times.

To thee, O Sacred Heart of Jesus,—to thee
I offer and devote my life, thoughts, words,
actions, pains, and sufferings. May the least
part of my being be no longer employed, save
only in loving, serving, honouring, and glorifying thee. Wherefore, O most Sacred Heart,
be thou the sole object of my love, the protector
of my life, the pledge of my salvation, and my
secure refuge at the hour of my death. Be
thou, O most bountiful Heart, my justification
at the throne of God, and screen me from his
anger, which I have so justly merited. In
thee I place all my confidence; and, convinced
as I am of my own weakness, I rely entirely on
thy bounty. Annihilate in me all that is dis-
pleasing and offensive to thee. Imprint thyself, like a divine seal, on my heart, that I may
ever remember my obligations, and never be
separated from thee. May my name also, I
beseech thee, be ever fixed and engraved in
thee, O Book of Life! May I ever be a victim

consecrated to thy glory, burning with the flames of thy pure love, and entirely penetrated with it for an eternity! In this I place all my happiness; this is all my desire, to live and die in no other quality than that of thy devoted servant.

Through thy Sacred Heart, O Jesus, overflowing with all sweetness, we recommend to thee ourselves, and all our concerns, our friends, benefactors, relations, superiors, and enemies. Take under thy protection this house, city, and kingdom; extend this thy care to all such as are under any affliction, and to those who labour in the agony and pangs of death; cast an eye of compassion on the obstinate sinner, and more particularly on the poor suffering souls in Purgatory; also on those who are united with us in the holy confederacy of honouring and worshipping thee. Bless these in particular, O bountiful Jesus; and bless them according to the extent of thine infinite goodness, mercy, and charity.

Act of Reparation

FOR THE FIRST FRIDAY OF THE MONTH.

O most amiable and adorable Heart of Jesus! centre of all hearts, glowing with charity, and inflamed with zeal for the interest of thy Father and the salvation of mankind! O Heart ever sensible of our misery, and ever in motion to redress our evils; the real victim of

love in the Holy Eucharist, and propitiatory
Sacrifice for sin on the altar of the Cross! seeing that the generality of Christians make no
other return for these thy mercies than contempt of thy favours, forgetfulness of their own
obligations, and ingratitude to the best of benefactors, is it not just that we thy servants,
penetrated with the deepest sense of the like
indignities, should enter upon a due and satis-
factory reparation of honour to thy most sacred Majesty? Prostrate, therefore, in body,
and humbled in mind before heaven and earth,
we solemnly declare our utter detestation and
abhorrence of such conduct. Inexpressible,
we know, was the bitterness which the multitude of our sins brought on thy tender Heart;
insufferable the weight of our iniquities, which
pressed thy face to the earth in the Garden of
Olives; and insurmountable thy anguish, when,
expiring with love, grief, and agony on Mount
Calvary, in thy last breath thou wouldst re-
claim sinners to their duty and repentance.
This we know, O dear Redeemer; and would
most willingly redress these thy sufferings by
our own, or share with thee in thine.

O merciful Jesus, ever present on our altars,
and with a heart open to receive all who labour
and are burdened! O adorable Heart of Jesus,
Source of true contrition, impart to our hearts
the true spirit of penance, and to our eyes a
fountain of tears, that we may bewail and wash
off our sins and those of the world. Pardon,
Divine Jesus, all the injuries, reproaches, and

outrages done thee through the course of thy
holy life and bitter Passion. Pardon all the
impieties, irreverences, and sacrileges which
have been committed against thee in the Sacrament of the Eucharist from its first institu-
tion. Graciously receive the small tribute of
our sincere repentance as an agreeable offering
in thy sight, and in requital for the benefits
we daily receive from the altar, where thou art a
living and continual Sacrifice, and in union of
that bloody Holocaust thou didst present to
thy eternal Father on Mount Calvary from the
Cross.

Sweet Jesus, give thy blessing to the ardent
desire we now entertain, and the holy resolution we have taken, of ever loving and adoring
thee after a proper manner in the Sacrament
of love, the Eucharist; thus to repair, by a true
conversion of heart and a becoming zeal for
thy glory, our past negligence and infidelity.
Be thou, O adorable Heart, who knowest the
clay of which we are formed,—be thou our
Mediator with thy Heavenly Father, whom we
have so grievously offended. Strengthen our
weakness, confirm our resolution, and, with
thy charity, humility, meekness, and patience,
cover the multitude of our iniquities. Be thou
our Support, our Refuge, and our Strength,
that nothing henceforth in life or death may
separate us from thee. Amen.

The Examen.

(Nine o'clock.)

Did I make the Examen this morning, and how did I make it?

How have I performed the duties since?—school, visiting the sick, &c.?

How did I observe the rule of silence?

Have I committed any faults against charity, humility, obedience, &c.?

Did I try to preserve recollection?

How have I said the Office, Rosary, and other vocal prayers?

Did I spend my leisure-time unprofitably, or have I given way to idle reflections?

How did I act at recreation?

Was I charitable, obliging, and kind to every sister?

Did I raise my heart to God from time to time?

How often have I visited the Blessed Sacrament?

How did I act in the refectory?

Make an act of contrition for your faults, promise to serve God more faithfully, and beg his grace.

Litany of the Saints.

Remember not, O Lord, our offences, nor those of our fathers; neither take thou vengeance of our sins.

Lord, have mercy.
Lord, have mercy.
Christ, have mercy.
Christ, have mercy.
Lord, have mercy.
Lord, have mercy.
Christ, hear us.
Christ, graciously hear us.

God the Father, of heaven,
God the Son, Redeemer of the world,
God the Holy Ghost,
Holy Trinity, one God,

Have mercy upon us.

Holy Mary,
Holy Mother of God,
Holy Virgin of virgins,
St. Michael,
St. Gabriel,
St. Raphael,
All ye holy Angels and Archangels,
All ye holy orders of blessed Spirits,
St. John Baptist,
St. Joseph,
All ye holy Patriarchs and Prophets,
St. Peter,
St. Paul,
St. Andrew,
St. James,
St. John,

Pray for us.

St. Thomas,
St. James,
St. Philip,
St. Bartholomew,
St. Matthew,
St. Simon,
St. Thaddeus,
St. Matthias,
St. Barnabas,
St. Luke,
St. Mark,
All ye holy Apostles and Evangelists,
All ye holy Disciples of our Lord,
All ye holy Innocents,
St. Stephen,
St. Lawrence,
St. Vincent,
SS. Fabian and Sebastian,
SS. John and Paul,
SS. Cosmas and Damian,
SS. Gervase and Protase,
All ye holy Martyrs,
St. Sylvester,
St. Gregory,
St. Ambrose,
St. Augustine,
St. Jerome,
St. Martin,
St. Nicholas,
All ye holy Bishops and Confessors,
All ye holy Doctors,
St. Anthony,
St. Benedict,

Pray for us.

St. Bernard,
St. Dominic,
St. Francis,
All ye holy Priests and Levites,
All ye holy Monks and Hermits,
St. Mary Magdalene,
St. Agatha,
St. Lucy,
St. Agnes,
St. Cicily,
St. Catherine,
St. Anastasia,
All ye holy Virgins and Widows,
All ye holy men and women, Saints of
   God,
Make intercession for us.
Be merciful,
Spare us, O Lord.
Be merciful,
Graciously hear us, O Lord.
From all evil,
From all sin,
From thy wrath,
From sudden and unlooked-for death,
From the snares of the devil,
From anger, and hatred, and every evil
   will,
From the spirit of fornication,
From lightning and tempest,
From everlasting death,
Through the mystery of thy holy Incarna-
   tion,
Through thy Coming,

Pray for us.

O Lord, deliver us.

Through thy Nativity,
Through thy Baptism and holy Fasting,
Through thy Cross and Passion,
Through thy Death and Burial,
Through thy holy Resurrection,
Through thine admirable Ascension,
Through the coming of the Holy Ghost the
    Paraclete,
In the day of judgment,
We sinners,
Beseech thee hear us.
That thou wouldst spare us,
That thou wouldst pardon us,
That thou wouldst bring us to true pen-
    ance,
That thou wouldst vouchsafe to govern and
    preserve thy holy Church,
That thou wouldst vouchsafe to preserve
    our Apostolic Prelate, and all orders of
    the Church in holy religion,
That thou wouldst vouchsafe to humble
    the enemies of holy Church,
That thou wouldst vouchsafe to give peace
    and true concord to Christian kings and
    princes,
That thou wouldst vouchsafe to grant peace
    and unity to all Christian people,
That thou wouldst vouchsafe to confirm and
    preserve us in thy holy service,
That thou wouldst lift up our minds to hea-
    venly desires,
That thou wouldst render eternal blessings
    to all our benefactors,

O Lord, deliver us.

We beseech thee, hear us.

That thou wouldst deliver our souls, and the souls of our brethren, relations, and benefactors, from eternal damnation,

That thou wouldst vouchsafe to give and preserve the fruits of the earth,

That thou wouldst vouchsafe to grant eternal rest to all the faithful departed,

That thou wouldst vouchsafe graciously to hear us,

We beseech thee, &c.

Son of God,

Lamb of God, who takest away the sins of the world,

Spare us, O Lord.

Lamb of God, who takest away the sins of the world,

Graciously hear us, O Lord.

Lamb of God, who takest away the sins of the world,

Have mercy on us.

Christ, hear us.

Christ, graciously hear us.

Lord, have mercy.

Christ, have mercy.

Lord, have mercy.

Our Father (*secretly*).

℣. And lead us not into temptation.

℟. But deliver us from evil.

Psalm lxix. *Deus in adjutorium.*

1 O God, come to my assistance: O Lord, make haste to help me.

2 Let them be confounded and ashamed: that seek after my soul.

3 Let them be turned backward, and blush for shame: that desire evils unto me.

4 Let them be straightway turned backward blushing for shame, that say unto me: 'Tis well, 'tis well.

5 Let all that seek thee be joyful and glad in thee: and let such as love thy salvation say always, The Lord be magnified.

6 But I am needy and poor: O God, help thou me.

7 Thou art my helper and my deliverer: O Lord, make no long delay.

Glory be, &c.

℣. Save thy servants.

℟. Who hope in thee, O my God.

℣. Be unto us, O Lord, a tower of strength.

℟. From the face of the enemy.

℣. Let not the enemy prevail against us.

℟. Nor the son of iniquity approach to hurt us.

℣. O Lord, deal not with us according to our sins.

℟. Neither requite us according to our iniquities.

℣. Let us pray for our Sovereign Pontiff, N.

℟. The Lord preserve him and give him life, and make him blessed upon the earth; and deliver him not up to the will of his enemies.

℣. Let us pray for our benefactors.

℟. Vouchsafe, O Lord, for thy name's sake, to reward with eternal life all them that do us good. Amen.

℣. Let us pray for the faithful departed.

℟. Eternal rest give unto them, O Lord, and let perpetual light shine upon them.

℣. May they rest in peace.

℟. Amen.

℣. For our absent brethren.

℟. Save thy servants, who hope in thee, O my God.

℣. Send them help, O Lord, from the sanctuary.

℟. And defend them out of Sion.

℣. O Lord, hear my prayer.

℟. And let my cry come unto thee.

Let us pray.

O God, whose property is always to have mercy and to spare, receive our humble petition; that we, and all thy servants who are bound by the chain of sins, may, by the compassion of thy goodness, mercifully be absolved.

Graciously hear, we beseech thee, O Lord, the prayers of thy suppliants, and forgive the sins of them that confess to thee; that, in thy bounty, thou mayest grant us both pardon and peace.

Show forth upon us, O Lord, in thy mercy, thy unspeakable loving-kindness; that thou mayest both loose us from all our sins, and deliver us from the punishments which we deserve for them.

O God, who by sin art offended, and by penance pacified, mercifully regard the prayers of thy people making supplication to thee, and turn away the scourges of thine anger, which we deserve for our sins.

Almighty, everlasting God, have mercy upon thy servant N, our Sovereign Pontiff, and direct him, according to thy clemency, into the way of everlasting salvation; that by thy grace he may both desire those things that are pleasing to thee, and perform them with all his strength.

O God, from whom all holy desires, all right counsels, and all just works do come, give unto thy servants that peace which the world cannot give; that both our hearts being devoted to the keeping of thy commandments, and the fear of enemies being removed, our times, by thy protection, may be peaceful.

Inflame, O Lord, our reins and heart with the fire of the Holy Ghost; that we may serve thee with a chaste body, and please thee with a clean heart.

O God, the Creator and Redeemer of all the faithful, give to the souls of thy servants departed the remission of all their sins; that through pious supplications they may obtain the pardon which they have always desired.

Prevent, we beseech thee, O Lord, our actions by thy inspirations, and further them with thy continual help; that every prayer and work of ours may always begin from thee, and through thee be likewise ended.

Almighty, everlasting God, who hast dominion over the living and the dead, and art merciful to all, who thou foreknowest will be thine by faith and works; we humbly beseech thee that they for whom we intend to pour forth our prayers, whether this present world still detain them in the flesh, or the world to come hath already received them, stripped of their mortal bodies, may, by the grace of thy loving-kindness, and by the intercession of all the Saints, obtain the remission of all their sins. Through thy Son Jesus Christ our Lord, who liveth and reigneth with thee, in the unity of the Holy Spirit, God, for ever and ever.

℟. Amen.

℣. O Lord, hear my prayer.

℟. And let my cry come unto thee.

℣. May the almighty and merciful Lord graciously hear us.

℟. Amen.

℣. And may the souls of the faithful, through the mercy of God, rest in peace.

℟. Amen.

Let us pray.

Visit, we beseech thee, O Lord, this habitation, and drive far from it all snares of the enemy. Let thy holy Angels dwell herein, to preserve us in peace; and may thy blessing be always upon us; through our Lord, &c.

Save us, O Lord, when we are awake, and keep us while we sleep; that we may watch with Christ, and rest in peace.

℟. Amen.

After night prayers, keep your mind attentive to the subject of the meditation read in choir, or some other pious consideration.

Take your rest in obedience to God's holy will, and in his Divine presence, modestly crossing your arms on your breast; and let your last action, like your first, be the sacred sign of the cross.

Before Noblceship.

" Come, Holy Ghost, take possession of our hearts, and kindle in them the fire of Divine love."

Direct, we beseech thee, O Lord, our actions by thy holy inspirations, and carry them on by thy gracious assistance, that every prayer and work of ours may always begin from thee, and by thee be happily ended. Through Jesus Christ our Lord. Amen.

" We fly to thy protection, O sacred Mother of God. Despise not our petitions in our necessities, but ever deliver us from all dangers, O ever-glorious and blessed Virgin."

℣. Pray for us, O holy Mother of God.

℟. That we may be made worthy of the promises of Christ.

O sacred Mother of God, blessed model of that perfection to which all are called who leave the world, take us under thy powerful protection, and preserve us from the misfortune of counteracting the merciful designs of our Redeemer over our souls ; offer our hearts to him who formed them for himself, and obtain for us the grace to imitate faithfully those admirable virtues thou didst practise during thy mortal life, particularly thy profound humility, perfect obedience, tender charity, and spirit of prayer and recollection. Amen.

Occasional Prayers.

FOR A SISTER IN RETREAT.

Almighty and most merciful God, we earnestly beg your grace and blessing for our sister in retreat. Assist her, we humbly beseech you, to accomplish your holy will; direct her particularly in what she is about to undertake, and teach her to act in the manner most pleasing to your Divine Majesty. Enlighten her by your wisdom, support her by your power, and by your infinite goodness direct all her exertions on this occasion, to your greater glory and her own eternal salvation. Amen.

FOR A SICK SISTER.

My God, look down with mercy and pity on our dear sister afflicted with sickness. Give her perfect resignation to your Divine will, and graciously enable her to suffer without complaining whatever you are pleased to appoint.

Compassionate Lord Jesus, support and comfort her.

Blessed Mother of God, and all you happy Saints, intercede for her, that she may pass through this time of trial so as to purify her heart from the smallest stain, that at the hour of her departure from this miserable world she may enter on the joys of a glorious eternity. Through Jesus Christ our Lord. Amen.

Prayers

FOR THOSE ENGAGED IN INSTRUCTION.

Thou, O Lord, art my Patience and my Strength ; thou art my Light and my Counsel ; thou subduest under me the children whom thou hast confided to my care ! Oh, leave me not one moment to myself, but give me, for the instruction of others, and for my own salvation, the spirit of wisdom and understanding, the spirit of counsel and strength, the spirit of knowledge and piety, and, above all, the spirit of the fear of the Lord. Amen.

O my Jesus, nothing for myself, but all for thee !

Divine Spouse of my soul, I will watch over the innocent, that they may never offend thee. I will teach thy ways to the unjust, that they may be converted to thee. I will instruct the ignorant, that they may know thee; and labour to inflame the tepid, that they may love thee. Every power and every affection of my heart and soul shall be for thee. Thou, who knowest all things,—thou knowest that the motive of even the least of my actions is thy love, and that I desire no recompense but the happiness of pleasing thee. Yes, adorable Jesus ! could I but induce one heart to love thee sincerely, the labours of ten thousand years would be superabundantly rewarded.

Sweet Jesus, would that I could speak most lovingly of thee! Would that I could teach the little ones thou didst so much cherish on earth how sweet a thing it is to love thee! how much they lose, by their want of fervour, their want of tenderness for thee! Well I know, my God, thou hast good and great gifts for all,—the old and the young, the repenting sinner, and the saint who has never offended thee; but the purest of all thy joys, the most treasured of all thy graces, thou dost reserve for the little child, who gives to thee the "morning prayer" of its young heart, and who has learned whilst yet its lips are pure, and its heart unstained by sin, to call devoutly on the Name of Jesus.

BEFORE ANY DUTIES OF CHARITY.

I offer, O my God, in union with the adorable actions and sufferings of Jesus Christ during his mortal life, the duties I am now going to perform for thy love and in obedience to thy most holy will. I most humbly beg thy Divine blessing, and the light of thy Holy Spirit, that all my duties and occupations may tend to thy greater glory and my eternal salvation, as likewise to the service and edification of my neighbour. Through Jesus Christ our Lord. Amen.

AN ACT OF FAITH BEFORE OUR DUTIES OF CHARITY.

O adorable Saviour! I firmly believe thou residest in the persons of the poor, and that in serving them I have the happiness of serving thee. Thou hast promised to be mindful on the day of final retribution of all that I shall have done in thy name to the least of thine. Increase in me, O God, the faith of this consoling promise, that my charity may become more ardent and more pure, may render me more pleasing in thy sight, and may merit for me a greater reward. Amen.

Remember, O most pious Virgin, it is a thing unheard of thou ever forsakest those who have recourse to thee. Encouraged with this hope and confidence, my most dear Mother, I, a most miserable sinner, cast myself at thy sacred feet, humbly begging that thou wilt adopt me as thy child for ever, and take upon thee the care of my eternal salvation. Do not, O Mother of the Word Incarnate, reject my petition, but graciously hear and grant it. Amen.

Humble my pride, O humble Jesus! May thy Divine Spirit become sensible to my miserable heart, and consume therein that innate root of pride, which increases and strengthens with me, which follows me every where, and insinuates itself into all my works, even the most holy. Extend thy arm, O Lord! Show me the power of thy grace, and confound my pride. Inspire me with a sincere hatred and contempt for myself, a cordial and intimate love of humility, that I may be worthy of being thy disciple, that I may love what thou lovest, follow what thou teachest, and shun pride, which thou abhorrest. Amen.

Dear Jesus! thou knowest what I now stand in need of; thou knowest the boon that I am most anxious to obtain. Oh, forgive me if I trust too firmly in thee, that I shall not pray in vain; forgive me if I remember that thou hast said, " Ask, and you shall receive; seek, and you shall find; knock, and it shall be open unto you." Behold, now I pray to thee; behold, now I seek, I knock, I ask. Grant me, oh, grant me my request, and let not my trust in thy blessed promise be disappointed : " Whatever you ask the Father in my name, it shall be granted unto you." Remember, great God, eternal Father, whom Christ thy Son has taught me to adore as my Father also in heaven,—remember this promise of my Redeemer, and fulfil my request. In his name, —in the name of Jesus Christ thy Son,—I beg of thee to hear my petition, and bestow on me this blessing. Redeem, great God, his promise, and enable me to ask that my faith may be strengthened and assured. Let me not be disappointed, O God, for I have trusted in Jesus Christ thy Son; who, with thee and the Holy Ghost, liveth and reigneth, one God, world without end. Amen.

O amiable and suffering Jesus, I fly to thee for protection. Hide me in thy sacred Wounds, and never permit me to leave thee in life or death. In the Wounds of thy sacred Feet I place my poverty, that I may learn of thee to trample under foot all earthly things. I place my obedience in the Wounds of thy sacred Hands, that I may learn of thee cheerfully to embrace and fulfil all that is enjoined me. In the precious Wound of thy sacred Side I place the tender lily of purity, that it may live in spotless beauty in the warm atmosphere of thy sacred Heart.

Prayer before Confession.

It is at thy sacred feet, O infinitely merciful Jesus, that I am now going to cast myself; let me be so happy as to find mercy and pardon, and may no evil disposition of mine be an obstacle to the grace of this Sacrament. I beseech thee to supply from the treasure of thine infinite merits all my deficiencies in preparing for it. Accept on my behalf, O sweet Jesus, the clear view thou hadst of all my sins in the Garden of Gethsemani, to supply for my imperfect knowledge of them, or any defect in my examination. I offer thee thy sighs, thy tears, thy fainting and bloody sweat, the bitter anguish which penetrated thy amiable heart, to supply for the weakness of my contrition. I offer thee thy merciful resolution of dying for the expiation of my sins to atone for any

deficiency in my determination of amendment.
O adorable heart of Jesus! which was sorrow-
ful even unto death for those very sins I am
about to accuse myself of; which was wounded
on the cross, and thus rendered the refuge of
sinners; remember all I have cost thee, and
apply to my soul abundantly the infinite merits
of thy humiliations, sufferings, and anguish.
Let thy Divine Spirit, O Lord, be in my heart
and on my lips, that my confession may be
sincere, entire, humble, and penitent. O Mother of God! Mother of mercy and refuge of
sinners! intercede for me, that this confession
I am going to make may not render me more
guilty, but may obtain for me the remission of
my sins, and grace to avoid them for the future. My good Angel and holy Patrons, I beseech you to assist me, that this confession
may tend to God's glory and my eternal salvation. Amen.

Prayer after Confession.

I beseech thee, O my dear Lord Jesus, by
thine infinite mercy, by the Immaculate Heart
of thy loving Mother, and by the merits of all
the Saints, graciously to accept this my confession. Let it be pleasing to thy Sovereign
Majesty and profitable to my soul. Let thine
infinite sweetness of love and bitterness of
sorrow supply all its defects; whether it be
want of contrition, of integrity, of humility, of
charity, of simplicity, of a true sense of the

heinousness of my sins, of a full resolution of amendment, or any other circumstance, negligence, or error whatsoever. Teach me, O Lord, how to persevere in thy love, and to correspond to my vocation with a zealous ardour, joined with prudence and discretion, that, serving thee, my Sovereign Lord and Master, during my abode in this prison of mortality, with fidelity, simplicity, and sincerity, I may at the end of my life be received into the mansions of immortality with security; and that, as I here justly sing forth thy mercies for having used such sweet and efficacious means for bringing my poor sinking soul into the safe haven, so I may there joyfully sing eternal canticles of Divine praises in thy kingdom of glory. Amen.

Offering of Penance.

My God, I offer thee the penance I am going to perform, together with whatever pain of mind or body I may suffer during the week, in union with the sufferings and satisfactions of my Divine Redeemer Jesus Christ, begging that the abundance of his merits, and the immense extent of his love and dolours, may supply the defects of all the satisfactions of which I stand indebted to thy Divine justice. Amen.

Behold, O Lord, this poor and miserable heart of mine, which through thy goodness has conceived many good resolutions, but which, alas, is, of itself, too wretched to execute the good which it desires, unless thou impart to it thy heavenly blessing, which, for this end, I humbly beg of thee, O most merciful Father, through the merits of the Passion of thy Son, to whose honour I consecrate every moment of my life.

O Heart of my Saviour! Divine Heart, of whose love I am unworthy, yet in whose mercy I unreservedly hope, in thee I place all my trust. Adorable source of charity, from thee I expect my pardon; for thou art deep enough to drown all my evils, ardent enough to consume all my offences, and afflicted enough to supply the defects of my imperfect contrition. Mortify in me, dear Jesus, all that displeases you, and make me according to your own heart's desire.

_____

Preparation for Communion.

1.

Holy Patriarchs and Prophets, Abraham, Moses, and David, who desired so earnestly the coming of the Saviour of the world, obtain for me of his Divine Majesty desires like yours, and all dispositions for receiving him worthily in the Holy Communion, for which I say from my inmost heart, Veni Domine Jesu Christe, et noli tardare. Come, Lord Jesus, take possession of my soul for ever by the Holy Com-

munion; hasten to come and make thyself
master of my mind and heart and all that I
am, that I may be thine in time and eternity.
Hasten, O Lord, to come into my soul; I desire thee ardently. Increase this desire in me,
and give me the purity thou wouldst have in
me.

2.

Sacred College of Apostles, who announced
the Gospel, perfect imitators of Jesus Christ,
St. Peter, St. Paul, and St. John, obtain for me
of that Divine Master a lively faith, a firm hope,
and an ardent charity to receive him worthily
in the Holy Communion, for which I say from
my inmost heart, Veni Domine Jesu Christe,
&c. O my soul, let us live by God and for
God, since he is pleased to make his abode in
us. Adorable Victim, oh, come, and delay no
longer!

3.

O glorious Martyrs, Confessors, and Virgins,
who exult for ever in heaven with Jesus Christ,
obtain for me of that Divine King strength to
conquer my vices, patience, and perfect purity
of heart, that I may be pleasing to his Divine
Majesty, to receive him worthily in the Holy
Communion. Veni Domine Jesu Christe, &c.
O Jesus, my Divine Spouse, come into me;
but first fill my soul with thy holy grace to receive thee well.

4.

Angels of heaven, St. Michael, St. Gabriel,
and St. Raphael, and my holy Angel Guardian,

who never cease to praise God, to love him, and
to fulfil his holy will, obtain for me the grace
of sharing in your great virtues to communicate worthily, that my heart may be the throne
of that Divine Master, and I may eternally
sing his mercies with you; that I may love
him and obey his holy law on earth to possess
him in heaven in your company. Veni Domine
Jesu Christe, &c. O my amiable Saviour, when
will the moment arrive that I shall be united
to you by the Holy Communion?

5.

Most holy and sacred Virgin; most worthy
Mother of God, advocate and refuge of sinners;
prostrate at thy feet, I implore thee to obtain
for me of thy dear Son, as dispositions for Holy
Communion, modesty, purity, humility, and
devotion, and to prepare my soul so well to receive the sacred Body of thy Divine Son Jesus,
that my heart may be to him an agreeable
dwelling, and that I may render him all the
glory I possibly can. Veni Domine Jesu Christe,
&c. O most holy Virgin, obtain for me of thy
dear Son humility and love of him, to receive
him and communicate worthily.

6.

O Comforter of souls, most Holy Spirit, pardon me the sins I have committed through
malice. Burn and consume my heart with the
fire of thy love, that I may be worthy to receive
within me Jesus Christ. Veni Domine Jesu

Christe, &c. O Holy Spirit, come to inflame my heart, or give me a new one, holily to receive Jesus Christ.

7.

O Son of Almighty God, increated Wisdom; prostrate before the throne of thy mercy, I implore thee, by the love thou bearest thy Father, to apply to me thy sacred merits. Wash away my sins in thy precious Blood, and do not permit me to receive thee unworthily. Come, O my amiable Jesus, to establish in my soul thy perpetual abode; and pardon me the sins I have committed through ignorance. Veni Domine Jesu Christe, &c. Come, Divine Saviour, the beloved of my heart; come to take possession of it for ever, thou who art the only object of my desires.

8.

Eternal Father, sovereign Power, Greatness, and Source of all perfection, I most humbly implore thee to purify my soul, and to make it a worthy abode for thy Divine Son, and to pardon me the sins I have committed through frailty. Veni Domine Jesu Christe, &c. Grant, O eternal Father, that thy only-begotten Son may possess my heart all the days of my life, with thee and the Holy Ghost. My heart is ready; O God, my heart is ready. My soul, penetrated with thy love, burns with the desire of receiving thee. O thou who art the source of its salvation! O expectation of nations! all desirable and so much desired! O fountain of living waters! when shall I approach thee to

E

quench my thirst in thy saving streams? Lord, I burn with thirst. Fountain of life, oh, satisfy this thirst! Sanctus! sanctus! sanctus!

Thanksgivings.

1.

What thanksgiving can I render thee, O Lord, in return for thy having given thyself to me in the adorable Sacrament of the Altar? Had I all the love of the seraphim, and of all the saints of heaven and just on earth, I should be incapable of thanking thee for so transcendent a benefit, were it not that I offer thee thyself. This I do most humbly for my whole thanksgiving, imploring thee, by the love which has induced thee to come to me, to grant me the grace of loving thee with my whole heart, and with a constant and unchangeable love. Laudate Dominum omnes gentes, &c.

2.

Only-begotten Son of God, why am I not perfect enough to thank thee worthily for the great mercy I have received from thee in the Holy Communion? But since I am incapable of it, I unite myself to thee, O my Divine Saviour, and offer thee the thanksgivings thou didst render thy Father at the moment of thy Incarnation and at the Last Supper, after thou hadst instituted this Divine Sacrament. Receive, O good Jesus, the avowal I make of my incapacity. Supply for my insufficiency, and remain eternally with me, thy poor child, who invites all creatures to praise and bless thee for ever. Laudate Dominum, &c.

3.

O God of mercy, I desire to praise thee and to thank thee for the benefit of Holy Communion as much as thou deservest, or at least as much as is in my power; but seeing that of myself I can do nothing, I offer thee that which is most agreeable to thee and most worthy of thee,—the love, the thanksgiving of thy Son my Saviour, and the offering he made thee of himself when he took upon him the work of our redemption; and implore thee most humbly, by the love which has induced thee to come and visit me, to remain eternally in me. Laudate Dominum, &c.

4.

O Mother of mercy, Refuge of sinners, and most holy Mother of my God, I have recourse, with all possible humility and confidence, to thy maternal goodness, to implore thee to thank thy dear Son for having so liberally given himself to me. Offer him, O holy Virgin, all the services thou renderedst him on earth, and all the thanksgivings thou didst return him when thou receivedst him, after his ascension, in the holy Sacrament, to satisfy for my sloth and tepidity. Laudate Dominum, &c.

5.

O my holy Angel Guardian, my faithful protector, thank my Divine Saviour for me for the favour he has done me in giving himself to me in this most holy Sacrament. O my good Angel, recommend my soul to his mercy, and obtain for me the graces necessary for my perfection and salvation. Laudate Dominum, &c.

6.

Glorious St. Joseph, faithful guardian of Jesus Christ, chaste spouse of the Blessed Virgin, look on me from the height of heaven, and pray to him for me, that he may leave nothing in my heart that can displease him; and that throughout life and death I may be penetrated with gratitude for his giving me himself in the Holy Communion; that he may strengthen me in the will he has given me of loving and imitating him the rest of my days; and that, by the favour of thy protection, God may grant me the grace of never offending him mortally. Laudate Dominum, &c.

7.

All my holy Patrons, and all you, Saints of God, resplendent with immortal glory in heaven, where you will for ever reign with God,— since you interest yourselves in my salvation, give thanks for me to his Divine Majesty for having given himself to my poor soul in the Holy Communion, and obtain for me perseverance in his holy service, even to the end. Laudate Dominum, &c.

Novenas in use amongst us.

FOR THE FEAST OF THE IMMACULATE CONCEPTION (DEC. 8TH).

O most pure and immaculate Virgin, who wert dignified by thy beloved Son with the most precious of all privileges,—an exemption from every stain of sin,—we commemorate with gratitude and joy that happy moment in which thou didst begin to live to grace. We return most ardent thanks to him who, in the instant of thy Immaculate Conception, began to do great things to thee. O incorruptible Ark! sacred Sanctuary! prepared to enclose the true Manna, the eternal Incarnate Word, let us, thy devoted clients, find a refuge in thee. Thou art the most privileged of all creatures,—the only one among the descendants of Adam who wert never for an instant an enemy of thy Creator. O most perfect image of the holiness of God, remember, we conjure thee, the ends for which thou wert enriched with graces, which no mortal before or since has ever enjoyed. Remember that thou wert miraculously preserved from a shadow of imperfection, not only that thou mightest become the Mother of God, but also the Mother, the Refuge, the Advocate of man. Penetrated, therefore, with the most lively confidence in thy never-failing mediation, we most humbly implore thy intercession for obtaining the intentions of this Novena.

Thou art, O sacred Mother of God, the Parent of virgins, and thereby the great Model of that sanctity which should adorn the spouses of Christ. To thee, then, we confidently recur, beseeching thee to obtain for us the grace to walk in thy footsteps. Thou knowest how often our hearts are the sanctuaries of a God who abhors iniquity. Obtain for us, then, that angelic purity which was thy earliest and favourite virtue,—that purity of heart which will attach us to God alone, and that purity of intention which will consecrate every thought, word, and action of our lives to his greater glory. Teach us to atone for our habitual imperfections by a fervent and habitual exercise of Divine love, and to endeavour, by fidelity to grace, to resist those sinful inclinations which never disturbed thy pure soul. Obtain for us chiefly a constant spirit of silence, prayer, and self-denial, that we may recover by penance that innocence which we lost by sin, and at length attain safely to that blessed abode of Saints, where nothing defiled can enter. Amen.

FOR CHRISTMAS.

O Son of the living God! O Desired of all nations! the Expectation, the Saviour of the world! do not permit that this solemnity, which transported the Angels with joy, and satisfied the longing desires of all the just, should pass without recalling to my mind the greatness of thy mercy, and the excess of that love which brought thee on earth.

O Word made flesh, and dwelling among us! O infinite Goodness, who wouldst rather save than condemn us! Eternal Greatness, who wouldst teach us to practise virtue by thy own example! Prostrate at thy crib, there will I dwell, for I have chosen it; or rather, O most beautiful above the sons of men! I present thee my heart, that thou mayest prepare it to become the crib of thy Nativity. I offer thee my memory, that it may dwell on the wonders of love which the manger of Bethlehem exhibits to the world. I offer thee my will, that the view of my Lord and Master, become subject to his own creatures, may totally destroy its perverse inclinations.

Oh, drop down dew, ye heavens, from above, and let the clouds rain the Just One; let the earth be opened, and bud forth a Saviour. O Brightness of eternal light! come and show us the vanity of all that the world calls great. Adorable Infant! sacred Babe of Bethlehem! in whose very name thy Saints have found inexpressible sweetness, I wish I could unite in my heart the faith of the ancient Patriarchs, the desires of the Just who preceded thy coming, the purity of the Angels who longed to announce thy birth, the tender love, the ineffable transports, which thy Infant Humanity has since excited in thy Saints; that thus I may invite thee with more fervour, and receive thee with less indignity into the cold, wretched mansion of my heart. But, my Sovereign Lord, though the dispositions of thy Angels and

Saints are far beyond my reach, yet I have a resource of which thou wilt not forbid me to profit. I unite my heart to thine, O adorable Treasure of all thy creatures! I desire to become thy sanctuary, in union with the eternal charity with which thou didst long to be born for man's redemption. I unite my heart to that of thy sacred Mother, and desire to receive thee with the transports of love with which she sighed to behold thee.

O most pure Mother of God, deign to prepare the dwelling of thy Infant Son in my heart; lay thy sacred Babe therein; but I entreat of thee, by the anguish thou didst endure from the cold and misery to which thou wert obliged to expose him at his birth, that his tears may soften my heart, his love inflame it, and his mercy adorn it with a share in the perfect dispositions of thy pure soul. Amen.

NOVENA TO ST. JOSEPH.

O glorious descendant of the kings of Judah! inheritor of the virtues of all the patriarchs! just and happy St. Joseph! listen to my prayer. Thou art my glorious protector, and shalt ever be, after Jesus and Mary, the object of my most profound veneration and tender confidence. Thou art the most hidden, though the greatest Saint, and art peculiarly the patron of those who serve God with the greatest purity and fervour. In union with all those who have ever been most devoted to thee, I now dedicate myself to thy service, beseeching thee, for the sake of

Jesus Christ, who vouchsafed to love and obey thee as a Son, to become a Father to me, and to obtain for me the filial respect, confidence, and love of a child towards thee. O powerful advocate of all Christians! whose intercession, as St. Teresa assures us, has never been found to fail, deign to intercede for me now, and to implore for me the particular intentions of this Novena. [*Specify them.*] Present me, O great Saint, to the adorable Trinity, with whom thou hadst so glorious and so intimate a correspondence. Obtain that I may never efface by sin the sacred image according to the likeness of which I was created. Beg for me that my Divine Redeemer would enkindle in my heart, and in all hearts, the fire of his love, and infuse therein the virtues of his adorable Infancy, his purity, simplicity, obedience, and humility. Obtain for me likewise a lively devotion to thy Virgin Spouse, and protect me so powerfully in life and in death that I may have the happiness of dying, as thou didst, in the friendship of my Creator, and under the immediate protection of the Mother of God.

Lord, have mercy on us.
Christ, have mercy on us.
Lord, have mercy on us.
Holy Trinity, one God, have mercy on us.
Holy Mary, Spouse of St. Joseph,
St. Joseph, confirmed in grace,
St. Joseph, Guardian of the Word Incarnate,

Pray for us.

St. Joseph, Favourite of the King of Heaven,

St. Joseph, Ruler of the Family of Jesus,

St. Joseph, Spouse of the ever-blessed Virgin,

St. Joseph, Nursing-father to the Son of God,

St. Joseph, Example of humility and obedience,

St. Joseph, Mirror of silence and resignation,

St. Joseph, Patron of innocence and youth,

St. Joseph, exiled with Christ into Egypt,

St. Joseph, Intercessor for the afflicted,

St. Joseph, Advocate of the humble,

St. Joseph, Model of every virtue,

St. Joseph, honoured amongst men,

St. Joseph, Union of all Christian perfection,

Pray for us.

Lamb of God, who takest away the sins of the world,

Spare us, O Lord.

Lamb of God, who takest away the sins of the world,

Graciously hear us, O Lord.

Lamb of God, who takest away the sins of the world,

Have mercy on us.

℣. Pray for us, O holy St. Joseph.

℟. That we may be made worthy of the promises of Christ.

Let us pray.

Assist us, O Lord, we beseech thee, by the

merits of the Spouse of thy most holy Mother,
that what our unworthiness cannot obtain may
be given us by his intercession with thee, who
livest and reignest, world without end. Amen.

FOR THE ANNUNCIATION OF THE BLESSED VIRGIN.

O admirable Virgin! the most exalted, yet
the most humble of all creatures! I salute
thee, in union with the respect and veneration
of the Angel who was deputed from heaven to
hail thee, full of grace, and to choose thee for
the Mother and Sanctuary of the Author of
all grace.

O most happy Mother! most pure Virgin!
most favoured among all women! why cannot
I join with the generations yet unborn "which
will call thee blessed"? why cannot I share in
the profound feelings of humiliation which
filled thy soul, even in the moment of thy glorious exaltation? O most humble, but most
privileged "handmaid of the Lord," since thou
hast found grace before God, obtain for me
that invaluable treasure, and fidelity to practise
all it requires. Since thou hast never felt the
anguish which springs from sin, and wert never
degraded by a single imperfection, thou hast
no cause to fear those tremendous judgments
which certainly await me if I continue to lead
an imperfect, tepid life in the sanctuary of religion. O powerful Protectress of those who
trust in thee! O Refuge of sinners! whose
misfortunes thou well knowest how to compas-

sionate, shield me from the anger of thy Divine Son; and since it is by thee he comes to us, may we, by thee, attain the enjoyment of his adorable presence in heaven.   Amen.

Devotions for the Month of May.

ACT OF CONSECRATION.

O most august and blessed Virgin Mary! holy Mother of God! glorious Queen of Heaven and earth! powerful Protectress of those who love thee, and unfailing Advocate of all who invoke thee! look down, we beseech thee, from thy throne of glory on us, thy devoted children. Accept the solemn offering we present thee of this month, especially dedicated to thee, and receive our ardent, humble desire, that by our love and fervour we could worthily honour thee, who, next to God, art deserving of all honour. Receive us, O Mother of Mercy, among thy best-beloved children; extend to us thy maternal tenderness and solicitude; obtain for us a place in the Heart of Jesus, and a special share in the gifts of his grace. Let not one perish of those that call thee their Mother, and look up to thee as their perfect model; permit not that this Community, which considers thee as its first Superior, should ever relax from the perfect observance of rule, or depart from exact adherence to the spirit of the holy institute we profess. Watch over, we

beseech thee, the spiritual and temporal inter-
ests of this thy little flock, and deign to recog-
nise its claims on thy powerful protection.
Obtain that we may be animated by the spirit
of union and charity, fervour and regularity,
humility, self-renunciation, and submission to
the holy will of God; that our hearts may burn
with the love of thy Divine Son, and of thee,
his blessed Mother, not for a month alone, but
for time and eternity. May we thirst for the
promotion of his honour and thine, and contri-
bute as far as we can to its extension.

Receive us, O Mary, Refuge of sinners, under
thy protection, and also the poor and children
committed to us; grant to each a mother's
blessing and a mother's care, now and at the
hour of death. Amen.

Most holy and most worthy Mother of God,
Queen of Heaven and earth, Daughter of the
Father, Mother of the Son, Spouse of the Holy
Ghost, Temple of the most august Trinity, Refuge of sinners and of all who hope in thee;
behold, we prostrate at thy feet, filled with inexpressible regret for all the faults we have
been guilty of in thy service; most humbly
beg pardon for them, and desire sincerely to
amend. We promise, in presence of the most
Holy Trinity and of all the Heavenly Court, to
take thee as our special Mother, Lady, and Advocate; beseeching thee with our whole hearts
to take under thy particular protection the go-
vernment of this Community, who choose thee

as their first and principal Superioress, and who are resolved to honour thee by their most humble respect and homage. And I, Sister N. N., though most unworthy, place this charge in thy hands, wishing henceforward to hold it but from thee, and subjecting myself, with this entire house, to thy guidance and direction, to render thee the homage, reverence, and obedience which we owe thee in quality of thy unworthy subjects and children. We have recourse with confidence to thy merciful protection, that thou mayest obtain for us grace to become all that thy Divine Son desires us to be ; most humbly beseeching thee to impart to each and every one of us thy holy benediction, and to assist us by thy special protection at the hour of our death. Amen.

℣. Nos cum prole pia.

℟. Benedicat Virgo Maria.

FOR THE LAST DAY OF MAY.

O sacred Heart of Mary ! noblest work of the Deity, Temple of the adorable Trinity, Sanctuary of charity, and unspotted Mirror of the Omnipotent sanctity ; Heart always sus· ceptible of the impulses of Divine love, and submissive to the Holy Spirit; which has extended thy affectionate solicitude from heaven to earth, from the just to sinners. ·

Heart always enriched with the friendship of Jesus, and by thy angelic sweetness delighting all thy favoured clients! Heart always honoured by the Angels in the heavenly Jeru-

salem, and continually blessed by the members
of the Church militant! Heart of a Mother,
next to God the most cherished object of our
veneration and devotion! Permit us, humbly
prostrate before thee, to present our fervent
petitions and homage. Holy Virgin, it is to
thee and to the love with which thy heart is
replenished that we are indebted for the singular privilege of having been called to religion,
as also for the many efficacious graces which
have been so liberally dispensed to us within
this sacred retreat; and to thee, O immaculate
Mother, we are specially indebted for all the
favours received during the precious month
which has just elapsed. How shall we thank
thee adequately for such innumerable blessings?

Incapable of presenting an offering worthy
of thy acceptance, we offer as a tribute of our
present gratitude all the honours paid to thee
by the blessed spirits, all the protestations of
love presented to thee by the most fervent souls
during this month dedicated to thy holy honour, as well as all the canticles of praise which
will be recited in thy honour during never-ending ages by Angels and men. O sacred Heart
of our Mother, nearly resembling that of Jesus,
which has been so often to us an asylum, a refuge, a temple, and a sanctuary, be propitious
to our supplications, and welcome us anew to
thy glorious haven; for if deprived of thy mediation, we shall not be enabled to triumph
over our spiritual enemies, or to fulfil the obli-

gations which we have contracted at the foot of thy altar.   Make us holy, O most holy of Virgins ; render us, like thee, poor in spirit and in truth, that we may make of our bodies and wills an offering sovereignly pleasing to the Lord.   Teach us to become meek and humble of heart, and in other respects imitators of our Divine Spouse; so that, like thee, by being perfectly dead to self, we may live henceforward for God alone.

Sacred Heart of Mary, receive us, protect us, assimilate us to thy Divine Son ; so that, having reposed during life under the shadow of thy protection, we may deserve to contemplate thee unceasingly in the mansions of eternal bliss.   Amen.

For Corpus Christi.

O amiable Jesus ! who hast given us in the adorable Eucharist so convincing a proof of thy infinite love, permit us to thank thee, in the name of all thy creatures, for the blessings included in this one precious gift.   We adore thee, O hidden Deity, and most ardently wish we could offer thee such love as would atone for our own offences and those committed by all mankind against this most amiable mystery.   But, my God, if all creatures are so deeply indebted to thy mercy for this adorable Sacrament, how much more sensibly should we feel our obligations, since by thy special predilection we have been chosen to dwell

under the same roof with thyself, to see thee
daily offered on our altars, and to receive so
frequently thy precious Body and Blood.
Convinced by these thy tender mercies that our
confidence in thy goodness cannot be too great,
we come now to implore of thee, by that infinite love which induced thee to institute this
adorable Sacrament, and by all the graces which
have ever flowed from this source of every blessing, to grant us the favour we ask in this Novena.

We firmly purpose to become from this moment the devoted adorers of this Sacrament of
love, and to take thy eucharistic life for the
rule and model of ours. Give us grace to honour thy silence on our altar by the spirit of
recollection and prayer; thy poverty, obedience, and adorable sanctity, by detachment from
all things, renunciation of self-will, and horror
of sin; above all, we beseech thee, O living
Bread of eternal life! to remove all obstacles
to our frequently and worthily receiving thee,
and to grant us so tender a devotion to this
amiable mystery that our hearts and thoughts
may ever be turned to thee present on our
altars, and every action of our lives be directed
to the perfect accomplishment of thy holy will.
Amen.

To be daily said during the month of June.

We adore, praise, and love thee, O sacred
Heart of our loving Jesus! and, full of grief at
the thought of so many offences which hitherto

F

have been, and still are, committed against thee
in the most holy Sacrament of the Altar, we
offer up the most amiable Heart of thy most
beloved Mother, with the merits of the Saints,
in satisfaction thereof. O sweet Jesus, enclose
in thy sacred Heart, we implore thee, all the
members of this Community ; and grant that,
faithfully observing our holy rule and our vows,
and complying fervently with the duties of our
holy state, we may be daily more and more
inflamed with Divine love, and praise thee
with unceasing gratitude for an endless eternity. Amen.

For the Feast of the Sacred Heart.

O adorable Jesus! who hast discovered to
us thy most Sacred Heart, that we may form
some idea of the extent of thy love, send forth
thy light and thy grace into our hearts, that
we may value as we ought so precious a favour.
We adore thee, O infinitely amiable Heart, and
beseech thee to receive our adorations, in unison with those thou thyself renderest to the
Divinity on our altars, in unison with the perfect homage of all thy saints, and, in particular,
in unison with the unceasing adorations of the
heavenly spirits, who crowd thy sanctuary during this glorious solemnity, and honour the
presence of thy amiable Heart on our altars.
Yet it is not for those pure and ardent spirits
that thou burnest with love in the Holy Eucha-

rist; it is for us, it is for all creatures, even for those who are most unmindful of all thy mercies. But though all the world should forget thee, O Divine Victim of charity, surely we, at least, should return thee love for love, since thou hast loved us with an eternal charity, and selected us long before our existence as the favourites of thy Divine Heart, the objects of its tenderest affection and peculiar favours. Penetrated with the confidence which should arise from the recollection of all thou hast already done for us, and art willing to do for those who trust in thee, we humbly represent our present necessities to thee, O adorable Heart, the Fountain of all grace, the Ocean of mercy, and exhaustless Source of consolation and strength! We most fervently entreat thee to infuse into our hearts the dispositions thou requirest, and then, for thy own sake, to grant the earnest petitions of this Novena.

Thou art, O Furnace of love, a public Victim. Thy mercies and graces are now peculiarly offered to all who will only ask, that they may receive; but thy tenderest compassion seems peculiarly directed to all unhappy sinners. For them thou wert overwhelmed with sorrow in the Garden of Olives, and wounded on the cross; for them we most particularly pray, and most earnestly entreat the grace of conversion. For ourselves, and every member of this Community, we beg the true spirit of our holy state, whatever particular graces thou knowest to be most necessary for each of us;

but particularly that ardent charity and sincere humility which seem to have been the favourite virtues of thy adorable Heart. Animate us with thy zeal for the salvation of those committed to our care; model their young hearts on thine, and assist us all to learn of thee, who art meek and humble of heart, that thereby we may find rest to our souls in this life, and everlasting repose in a happy eternity.

For the Feast of Pentecost
AND THE TEN PRECEDING DAYS.

O Jesus, triumphant conqueror of sin and death, who hast taken possession of that seat of bliss purchased by thy Blood, remember thy tender promise that thou wouldst not leave us orphans; send down upon us, and upon thy whole Church, that spirit of light, of truth, and of love, who alone can bring to our minds, and imprint on our hearts, the Divine lessons of humility, poverty, obedience, and contempt of the world, which thou hast taught us during thy mortal life. But, alas, if thy Apostles themselves were rendered unworthy of receiving the plenitude of thy Spirit, by too natural an attachment to thy adorable humanity, which was so lovely, so amiable, so deserving of their tenderest love, how can we hope for his descent into our hearts, which are defiled by a thousand imperfect and sinful inclinations? O my God, if thou desirest to give us thy Divine Spirit, prepare thyself his dwelling in our souls; unite our hearts and affections to the ardent sighs and perfect dispositions with which thy blessed Mother and Apostles awaited his coming. And thou, O adorable Spirit, who breathest where thou wilt, deign to descend on us, who are here assembled in thy Name, and on all the members of thy Church, to which thou wilt teach all truth to the end of time. O Spirit of purity, Spirit of peace, whom the foulest stains of sin cannot resist, purify our souls, and infuse therein that peace which the world cannot give. Oh, rend the heavens, and come down, consoling Spirit! that, strengthened and encouraged by thee, we may faithfully comply with the duties of our holy state, embrace the cross in whatever shape it is presented, and study to accomplish the Divine will with the utmost perfection.

Hymn.

Come, Holy Ghost, send down those beams, &c.

For the Assumption of the Blessed Virgin.

O glorious Queen of all the heavenly host! whose sacred body, the immaculate temple of the Divinity, is now assumed into heaven, I unite my voice to the choirs of Angels who celebrate thy triumph. Winter is now past for thee, O fervent follower of thy crucified Son. In this world, like him, thou hadst not any part in its perishable possessions; but now all the treasures of heaven are thine; they are thine to enjoy, and thine to distribute, for thy intercession is now an infinite treasure to man, which they that use become the friends of God. Thou wert buried in obscurity in this valley of tears; but now thou art compared with the light, and art found before it. O Mother of God, elevated to the highest pinnacle of glory, should not thy triumphant exaltation encourage us to despise this world, and aspire after the next; for, O amiable Virgin, how short were thy sufferings on earth, yet for all eternity thou shalt be admired in the holy assembly; among the elect thou shalt have praise, and among the blessed thou shalt be blessed. Look down, then, with compassion on us poor banished children of Eve; draw our hearts after thee by filial confidence, and vigorous exertions to imitate thy virtues; above all, obtain for us true humility, which neither seeks nor values any earthly distinction,—poverty of spirit, purity of heart, that thirst after the strong and living God which can never be satisfied until his glory appears,—and such ardent love of our Divine Spouse, as may cause us to despise the whole world, and incessantly sigh after those eternal joys which the eye hath not seen, the ear heard, neither hath it entered into the heart of man. Amen.

For the Nativity of the Blessed Virgin.

O Mary, the channel of God's tenderest mercies to man, thou wert promised from the beginning of the world to crush the serpent's head, to bring forth the Redeemer of mankind. In thy sacred birth appears the dawn of that glorious day of grace for which all nations ardently sighed. O blessed Infant, already thou beginnest to accomplish the predictions of the prophets, and to satisfy the longing desires of the just; already thou hast conceived in thy heart, by the most perfect love, that adorable Being who was afterwards to be born of thee. O happy Virgin! who, on entering the world, didst become a victim of charity, perfectly and unreservedly submissive to the will of God, may I, even at the last hour of my life, be enriched with a share in the dispositions with which thy soul was adorned in thy earliest infancy. Thou art the dignified descendant of kings, patriarchs, and prophets; yet thy birth so little corresponds with thy rank, that even the commencement of thy life may liken thee to him whom thou wert destined to resemble in all things. Inspire me, then, by thy example and intercession, with that spirit of renunciation, detachment from the world, and self-contempt, which I promised at my baptism, but which I solemnly engaged to practise at my religious profession. Thou knowest the weakness of and perverse inclinations which I brought into the world, and which unhappily have gained strength with increasing years. I conjure thee, O immaculate Virgin, by the purity and sanctity of thy nativity, by the riches of grace and virtue, which the weakness of childhood then concealed in thee, to obtain for me strength to fulfil the duties of my exalted state, to coöperate with the graces of heaven, and to advance daily, and even hourly, towards that perfection to which I am bound to aspire. Amen.

Thirty Days' Prayer.

Ever-glorious and blessed Mary, Queen of virgins, Mother of mercy, hope and comfort of dejected and desolate souls; through that sword of sorrow which pierced thy tender heart, whilst thine only Son, Jesus Christ our Lord, suffered death and ignominy on the cross; through that filial tenderness and pure love he had for thee, grieving in thy grief, whilst from his cross he recommended thee to the care and protection of his beloved disciple St. John; take pity, I beseech thee, on my poverty and necessities; have compassion on my anxieties and cares; assist and comfort me in all my infirmities and miseries, of what kind soever. Thou art the Mother of mercies, the sweet comforter and only refuge of the needy and the orphan, of the desolate and afflicted. Cast, therefore, an eye of pity on a poor child of Eve, and hear my prayer; for since, in just punishment of my sins, I find myself encompassed by a multitude of evils, and oppressed with much anguish of spirit, whither can I fly for more secure shelter, O amiable Mother of my Lord and Saviour Jesus Christ, than under the wings of thy maternal protection? Attend, therefore, I beseech thee, with an ear of pity and compassion, to my humble and earnest request. I ask it through the mercy of thy dear Son; through that love and condescension wherewith he embraced our nature, when, in compliance with the Divine will, thou gavest thy consent; and whom, after the expiration of nine months, thou broughtest forth from thy chaste womb to visit this world, and bless it with his presence. I ask it through that anguish of mind wherewith thy beloved Son, our dear Saviour, was overwhelmed on the Mount of Olives, when he besought his eternal Father to remove from him, if possible, the bitter chalice of his passion. I ask it through the threefold repetition of his prayer in the Garden, from whence afterwards, with sorrowing steps and mournful tears, thou didst accompany him to the doleful theatre of his death and sufferings. I ask it through the wounds and sores of his virginal flesh, occasioned by the cords and whips wherewith he was bound and scourged, when stripped of his seamless garment, for which his executioners afterwards cast lots. I ask it through the scoffs and ignominies wherewith he was insulted; the false accusations and unjust sentence by which

he was condemned to death, and which he
bore with heavenly patience. I ask it through
his bitter tears and bloody sweat, his silence
and resignation, his sadness and grief of heart.
I ask it through the Blood which trickled from
his royal and sacred head, when struck with
his sceptre of a reed, and pierced with his
crown of thorns. I ask it through the excru-
ciating torments he suffered, when his hands
and feet were fastened with heavy nails to the
cross. I ask it through his vehement thirst,
and bitter potion of vinegar and gall. I ask
it through his dereliction on the cross, when
he exclaimed: *My God! my God! why hast
thou forsaken me?* I ask it through his mercy
extended to the good thief, and through his
recommendation of his precious soul and spirit
into the hands of his eternal Father before he
expired, saying, *It is finished.* I ask it through
the blood mixed with water which issued from
his sacred side when pierced with a lance, from
whence a plenteous stream of grace and mercy
has flowed to us. I ask it through his immaculate life, his bitter passion, and ignomi-
nious death on the cross, at which nature itself
was thrown into convulsions, by the bursting
of rocks, rending of the veil of the temple, the
earthquake, and darkness of the sun and moon.
I ask it through his descent into hell, where
he comforted the Saints of the old law with his
presence, and led captivity captive. I ask it
through his glorious victory over death, when
he rose again to life on the third day, and

through the joy which his appearance, for forty days after, gave to thee, his blessed Mother, his Apostles, and the rest of his disciples, when, in thine and their presence, he miraculously ascended into heaven. I ask it through the grace of the Holy Ghost, infused into the hearts of the Apostles, when he descended upon them in the form of fiery tongues, which inspired them with zeal for the conversion of the world, when they went forth to preach the Gospel. I ask it through the awful appearance of thy Son, at the last dreadful day, when he shall come to judge the living and the dead, and the world by fire. I ask it through the compassion he bore thee in this life, and the ineffable joy thou didst feel at thine assumption into heaven, where thou art eternally absorbed in the sweet contemplation of his Divine perfections. O glorious and ever-blessed Virgin! comfort the heart of thy suppliant, by obtaining for me [*here mention your request, under the condition of its being agreeable to the will of God*]. And as I am persuaded my Divine Saviour doth honour thee as his beloved Mother, to whom he can refuse nothing, so let me speedily experience the efficacy of thy powerful intercession, according to the tenderness of thy maternal affection, and his filial loving heart, who mercifully granteth the requests, and complieth with the desires, of those that love and fear him. Wherefore, O most blessed Virgin, besides the object of my present petition, and whatever else I may stand

in need of, obtain for me also of thy dear Son,
our Lord and our God, a lively faith, a firm
hope, a perfect charity, a true contrition of
heart, unfeigned tears of compunction, a sincere confession, an abstinence from sin, a love
of God and my neighbour, a contempt of the
world, and patience under all affronts and ignominies; nay, even, if necessary, an oppro-
brious death itself, for the love of my Saviour
Jesus Christ. Obtain likewise for me, O sacred
Mother of God, perseverance in good works, the
performance of good resolutions, the mortifi-
cation of self-will, a pious conversation through
life, and, at my last moments, a strong and sincere repentance, accompanied by such a lively
and attentive presence of mind as may enable
me to receive the last Sacraments of the Church
worthily, and die in thy friendship and favour.
Lastly, obtain, I.beseech thee, for the souls of
my parents, brethren, relations, and benefactors, both living and dead, life everlasting.
Amen.

For the Feast of our Blessed Lady of Mercy.

O most holy Virgin, who wert chosen by the
adorable Trinity from all eternity to be the
most pure Mother of Jesus, permit me, thy
humble and devoted client, to remind thee of
the joy thou didst receive in the instant of the
most sacred Incarnation of our Divine Lord,
and during the nine months thou didst carry
him in thy chaste womb. I wish most sin-

cerely that I could renew or even increase that joy by the fervour of my prayers.

O tender Mother of the afflicted, grant me, under my present necessities, that peculiar protection thou hast promised to those who devoutly commemorate this ineffable joy. Relying on the infinite mercies of thy Divine Son; trusting in that promise which he has made, that those who ask should receive; and penetrated with confidence in thy powerful prayers, I most humbly entreat thee to intercede for me, and to obtain for me the favours I petition for in this Novena, if it be the holy will of God to grant them; and if not, to ask for me whatever graces I stand most in need of. [*Here specify your requests.*] I desire by this Novena, which I now offer in thy honour, to prove the lively confidence I have in thy intercession. Accept it, I beseech thee, in honour of that supernatural love and joy with which thy sacred Heart was replenished during the abode of thy dear Son in thy womb; in veneration of which I offer thee the sentiments of my heart, and these nine Hail Mary's. [*Repeat the Hail Mary nine times.*]

O Mother of God, accept these salutations, in union with the respect and veneration with which the Angel Gabriel first hailed thee, full of grace. I wish most sincerely that they may become so many gems in the crown of thy accidental glory, which will increase in brightness to the end of the world. I beseech thee, O Comfortress of the afflicted, by the joy thou

didst receive in the nine months of thy preg-
nancy, to obtain for me the grant of the favours I have now implored through thy powerful intercession. For this end I offer thee all
the good works which have ever been performed in thy honour. I most humbly entreat
thee, for the love of the most amiable Heart
of Jesus, with which thine was ever so inflamed, to hear my humble prayers, and to obtain my requests.

O God, who, under the protection of the
glorious Mother of thy Son, was pleased that
the Order of Mercy should be instituted in thy
Church, for the relief of the suffering and the
instruction of the ignorant, vouchsafe so to
strengthen and enlighten those to whom thou
hast granted this holy vocation, that they may
faithfully and efficaciously dispense thy mercies
on earth, and thereby come to the enjoyment
of thy Divine presence in heaven. Through our
Lord Jesus Christ. Amen.

O immaculate and ever-glorious Mary! Mother of mercy! ever gracious, ever bountiful,
behold we, thy suppliants, prostrate before thee
in all humility, most earnestly implore thee to
be our protectress and advocate with God, to
obtain for us those graces and blessings wh·ch
may best conduce to his greater glory and our
own sanctification. More particularly we beseech thy intercession in behalf of this Institute, founded under thy invocation, for the
exercise of those works of mercy which Jesus

Christ, the almighty Son of God, did so love when on earth. Defend it, O Blessed Lady, against its enemies. May it extend and prosper; and may the worship of God, thy honour, and the welfare of his servants, be promoted wherever it is established throughout the world. May the unity of charity prevail in all our Communities, and all scandals be unheard of amongst us. May those whom thy Divine Son has made his spouses, by calling them from their homes and kindred to dispense his mercies to their fellow-creatures, possess the true spirit of their Divine vocation. May they in all things seek to be united to him and to thee; to advance in all perfection by the observance of their holy rule and their vows; to deny themselves and be conformable to God's holy will. Obtain for them an ardent and ever-increasing zeal for the functions of the Institute. May their zeal be blessed by God, and efficacious for the welfare of the suffering, the erring, and the ignorant. Preserve them from all illusions, and sustain them amidst temptations. Beseech our Lord to add to their numbers subjects capable of glorifying him by efficaciously labouring for their own sanctification in the service of the poor; and so enlighten and direct the several Superiors of the Institute, that they may neither admit nor retain any save those to whom he has granted a due vocation, with grace to act up to it. May the blessing of God and thy protection be with all whom the Sisters protect and instruct.

Comfort and defend our parents, relations, and friends, and bring them to the enjoyment of eternal life with all our benefactors. That thou canst obtain for us these benefits, we know, O holy Mother of God; and we have filial confidence that thou wilt be favourable to us, because thou art the Mother of mercy, our Mother, and our patroness. Amen.

For the Feast of the Angel Guardians.

O pure and happy spirits, whom the Almighty selected to become the Angels and Guardians of men, I most humbly prostrate before you, to thank you for the charity and zeal with which you execute this commission. Alas, how many pass a long life without ever thanking that invisible friend, to whom they a thousand times owed its preservation! O charitable guardians of those souls for whom Christ died! O burning spirits, who cannot avoid loving those whom Jesus eternally loved! permit me to address you on behalf of all those committed to your care, and to implore for them all in general a grateful sense of your many favours, and also the grace to profit of your charitable assistance. O Angels of those happy infants who as yet are without spot before God, preserve their innocence, I earnestly conjure you. Angels of youth, who are exposed to so many dangers, conduct them safely to the bosom of God, as Tobias was conducted back to his father. Angels of those who employ themselves in the instruction of youth, animate them with your zeal and love; teach them to emulate your purity and incessant view of God, that they may worthily and successfully coöperate with the invisible guardians of their young charge. O Angels of the clergy, who have the eternal Gospel to preach to them that sit upon earth, present their words, their actions, and their intentions to God, and purify them in that fire of love which consumes you. Angels of those who are destined to follow the Lamb whithersoever he goeth, obtain for them the true spirit of their holy state, particularly the spirit of silence, recollection, and prayer, that in life and death they may be worthy to be united to their heavenly Spouse. Angels of infidels, whom the true faith has never enlightened, intercede for them, that, practising what they know, they may at length discover the hidden secrets of the kingdom of God. O Angels of all those who throughout the world are deprived of religious instruction, open for them some source of salvation; raise up some one to break for them the bread of the word. And you, O Guardian Angels of sinners, charitable guides of those unhappy mortals, whose perseverance in sin would embitter even your unutterable joys, were you not established in the peace of God,—oh, join me, I ardently beseech you, in imploring their conversion. Angels of all those who at this moment struggle in the agonies of death, strengthen, encourage,

G

and defend them against the attacks of their
infernal enemy. O faithful guides! holy spirits! ardent adorers of the Divinity! guardian
angels of all creatures! protect us all; teach
us to love, to pray, to combat on earth, and
rather obtain for us an instant death than
permit us to commit one mortal sin. Amen.

For the Presentation of the Blessed Virgin.

O incomparable Virgin! destined from all
eternity to become the living temple of the
Most High, permit thy devoted clients to remind thee of that entire, fervent, and most
perfect oblation which thou didst offer of thyself on the day of thy Presentation in the
Temple. O sacred model of those who are
called to leave all and follow Christ! Thou
art that Virgin by excellence, whose innocence
and sanctity were never defiled. To thee, then,
it peculiarly belongs, not only "to follow the
Lamb whithersoever he goeth," but also to
"lead many virgins in thy train." Oh, receive
us into the happy number of those whom thy
glorious example has urged to the heroic practice of religious perfection; obtain for us a
share in the dispositions of thy heart, when,
though a child in years, thou wert already far
advanced in eminent holiness, and, "forgetting
thy people and thy father's house," didst enter
the Temple to live to God, and for him alone.
We beseech thee, by the singular graces be-

stowed on thee then, to employ thy powerful interest in our behalf, and to obtain for us the intentions of this Novena.

Remember, O sacred Virgin, that thy early flight from the world, thy spirit of sacrifice and religious perfection in thy childhood, were all graces which entitle thee no less to our tender confidence than veneration. Listen, then, to the petitions we now make, and obtain for us also the true spirit of an interior life, that the Heart of Jesus may be henceforward our refuge and ordinary dwelling; teach us to commemorate thy consecration of thyself to God on the day of thy Presentation by a fervent renewal of our vows; that, after thy example, we may leave all in heart and will, and find all in Christ; that we may love God ardently, and all creatures for his sake; that his adorable will may be ours, and that every exertion of our mind and body may be happily consecrated to the promotion of his greater glory. Amen.